JOSH STEVE

Guardians of the Digital Age

Copyright © 2023 by Josh Steve

All rights reserved. No part of this publication may be reproduced, stored or transmitted in any form or by any means, electronic, mechanical, photocopying, recording, scanning, or otherwise without written permission from the publisher. It is illegal to copy this book, post it to a website, or distribute it by any other means without permission.

This novel is entirely a work of fiction. The names, characters and incidents portrayed in it are the work of the author's imagination. Any resemblance to actual persons, living or dead, events or localities is entirely coincidental.

Josh Steve asserts the moral right to be identified as the author of this work.

First edition

This book was professionally typeset on Reedsy.
Find out more at reedsy.com

Contents

The Virtual Encounter	1
The Profile Mystery	4
The First Date	8
The Disappearing Act	12
Unraveling the Deception	16
Digital Detectives	20
The Trail of Secrets	24
The Unraveling Truth	30
The Pursuit of Power	35
The Unveiling	40
The Balance of Power	44
The Final Confrontation	49

The Virtual Encounter

The streetlights flickered as rain poured down in relentless sheets, painting the night in a hazy, watery glow. Inside the cozy, dimly lit cafe, Julia sat nervously at a corner table, her fingers tapping an anxious rhythm on the porcelain cup before her. Her heart raced with the anticipation of what was about to unfold.

Tonight marked a pivotal moment in her life, a moment she had been both eager and terrified to embrace. After years of failed relationships and heartbreaks, Julia had decided to take the plunge into the world of online dating.

She took a deep breath, her hazel eyes darting around the cafe, scanning the faces of the few patrons who braved the storm. Her phone rested on the table, its screen illuminated with the dating app she had spent weeks deliberating over.

The digital age had ushered in a new era of romance, and Julia was determined to find love, or at the very least, a connection that resonated with her lonely heart.

Swiping right on profiles had felt impersonal, like flipping through a catalog of faces and bios. But then, a notification had flashed across her screen. A match. It had taken her by surprise, and she had been drawn to the enigmatic profile of a man named Daniel. His photo revealed only a fraction of his face, obscured by shadows, but there was something captivating about his dark eyes and the hint of a smile playing at his lips.

Messages had been exchanged, each word stoking the embers of excitement within her. Daniel had suggested they meet in person, to move beyond the pixels and discover if their connection transcended the digital realm.

Julia's phone buzzed, snapping her from her thoughts. Her heart leaped as she glanced at the screen. A message from Daniel. He was on his way. Her pulse quickened, and she couldn't help but wonder if he would be anything like his online persona.

Minutes stretched into eternity, and the anxiety gnawed at her. Had she made a mistake by agreeing to meet a stranger in a deserted cafe on a stormy night? She chastised herself for her recklessness and glanced at the entrance, her breath hitching as the door swung open, and a figure stepped inside, drenched from the rain.

Julia's eyes locked onto him, and her heart skipped a beat. It was him—Daniel. Tall and lean, his black coat clinging to his frame as droplets cascaded from his tousled hair. His eyes, as dark and captivating as they had appeared in his profile photo, found hers, and a lopsided grin tugged at his lips.

He approached her table, the soft murmur of raindrops serving as a backdrop to their meeting. Julia's nerves were eclipsed by a growing curiosity about this mysterious man who had managed to pull her from her solitary world.

"Julia?" he asked, his voice a low, melodic rumble that sent shivers down her spine.

She nodded, a shy smile curving her lips. "Yes, I'm Julia."

He extended his hand, and she reached out to shake it. His grip was firm but not overpowering, and his touch ignited a spark of electricity that shot through her.

"Daniel," he said, still smiling, and took a seat across from her.

The awkwardness of the initial meeting hung in the air for a moment before they both chuckled, breaking the tension. The conversation flowed naturally, as if they had known each other for ages. They talked about their lives, their passions, and their shared love for obscure indie films.

As minutes turned into hours, the world outside the cafe faded away, leaving only the two of them engrossed in each other's stories. Julia felt herself drawn deeper into Daniel's magnetic presence, his laughter a soothing melody in the midst of the storm.

Their empty cups and the cafe's dwindling number of patrons went unnoticed as they continued to talk, to laugh, and to connect. For the first time in a long while, Julia felt the warmth of companionship, the flicker of something more than just a casual encounter.

As the rain continued to dance on the windows, Julia and Daniel leaned closer, their words growing softer, more intimate. The chemistry between them was undeniable, an undeniable force that had transcended the boundaries of the digital age.

Outside, the storm raged on, but inside that little cafe, the world had narrowed to two souls navigating the uncharted territory of newfound connection. Julia's heart swelled with hope, and in that suspended moment, she knew that this virtual encounter had the potential to change the course of her life forever.

The Profile Mystery

The days following Julia's captivating encounter with Daniel at the rain-soaked cafe were a whirlwind of emotions. They had parted that night with promises to meet again soon, and their connection had grown stronger with each passing message and phone call.

Julia couldn't help but feel like she was living in a dream. The lonely nights and countless disappointments of the past had faded into a distant memory, replaced by the excitement and anticipation of what the future might hold.

As she sat in her cozy apartment one evening, her laptop open in front of her, Julia decided to delve deeper into the enigmatic world of Daniel. She had known him for just a short while, yet she couldn't shake the feeling that there was more to him than met the eye.

She opened the dating app on her laptop and navigated to Daniel's profile. The profile picture remained unchanged—a shadowy figure with those intense, dark eyes. Julia couldn't help but wonder why he was so insistent on maintaining his mysterious persona.

With a few clicks, she began her quest for answers. Julia had always been a curious person, and the more she connected with Daniel, the more her curiosity had grown. She was determined to uncover the man behind the shadows.

Her search led her to scan through his profile, reading between the lines of the brief description he had provided. "Lover of art, adventure, and the thrill of discovery," it read. It was cryptic, to say the least, and it only fueled her desire to know more.

Julia decided to take a closer look at the photos he had posted. The first image was the same one she had seen when they matched—a close-up of his face, half-hidden in darkness. The second photo, however, was different. It showed him standing on a cliff overlooking a vast, fog-shrouded valley. He was wearing a black leather jacket, his back to the camera, staring out into the distance.

The third photo was even more intriguing. It depicted Daniel in an art gallery, admiring a painting. The artwork was an abstract masterpiece, a riot of colors and shapes that seemed to reflect the chaos and beauty of life itself. Julia couldn't help but wonder about the significance of this particular image.

Her investigative instincts kicked into high gear. She had already learned that Daniel was a man of few words when it came to revealing personal details. But perhaps, she thought, there were clues hidden within the photos themselves.

Julia downloaded the images to her computer and opened a new browser tab. She began a reverse image search, hoping to find any online matches that might shed light on Daniel's true identity. The results were a mix of unrelated images and stock photos, none of which provided any meaningful information.

Frustrated but undeterred, Julia decided to dig deeper into his social media presence. She had his first name and a few details about his interests. It was a long shot, but she started searching for Daniel on various platforms, scouring profiles and timelines in search of a connection.

Hours turned into late-night exhaustion, but Julia's determination didn't waver. She was determined to unravel the mystery of Daniel. Finally, in a remote corner of the internet, she stumbled upon a forum post that caught her eye.

The post was on an obscure art discussion board, and the username caught her attention—DanielArtExplorer. Julia clicked on the post, her heart pounding as she read the words on the screen.

"I stumbled upon this breathtaking abstract painting today at a local gallery. The way it captures the chaos and beauty of life is truly mesmerizing. Art has the power to connect us to the depths of our souls, to emotions we can't put into words."

It was unmistakably Daniel's writing, and it was a post from several years ago. Julia's mind raced. She had uncovered a clue—a breadcrumb that led her closer to understanding the man she had met in the cafe.

With newfound determination, she continued to scroll through the forum. The more she read, the more she discovered about Daniel's passion for art and adventure. He had shared stories of his travels, of hidden gems he had stumbled upon, and of the thrill of discovery.

Julia's heart raced as she connected the dots. The mysterious man she had met on the dating app was more than just a stranger. He was a seeker of the extraordinary, an explorer of the unknown, and a connoisseur of art that touched the soul.

But one question remained—why had he hidden this side of himself behind a shroud of darkness and secrecy? What had he been searching for in the digital realm of online dating, and what had led him to her?

The puzzle pieces were falling into place, and Julia knew that her journey into the depths of the digital age was far from over. She had uncovered the first layer of Daniel's mystery, and it was a layer that only made her more intrigued by the enigmatic man she had come to know.

As the clock ticked into the early hours of the morning, Julia leaned back in her chair, a mixture of excitement and uncertainty coursing through her veins. She had embarked on a thrilling adventure, one that promised to take her to places she had never imagined, both in the real world and the digital realm. Daniel had ignited a spark within her, a spark that would drive her to uncover the secrets of the man behind the profile and to explore the uncharted territory of love in the digital age.

The First Date

A sense of trepidation mingled with excitement as Julia prepared for her second encounter with Daniel. Their digital connection had deepened in the days since their initial meeting at the rain-soaked cafe. Messages and phone calls had flowed effortlessly between them, building a sense of familiarity that belied the short time they had known each other.

Tonight was the night they had agreed upon for their second date, and Julia couldn't help but feel a flutter of nerves. Would their connection in person match the intensity of their online interactions? Or would the magic dissipate, leaving behind the specter of disappointment?

She stood before her bedroom mirror, scrutinizing her reflection. Julia had chosen a simple yet elegant black dress, a conscious nod to the shadowy aura that seemed to surround Daniel. Her hazel eyes were accentuated with a subtle smoky eye, and her heart-shaped face framed by loose waves of chestnut hair.

The minutes ticked away, each one bringing her closer to the appointed time. She couldn't shake the feeling that there was something extraordinary about Daniel, something that transcended the ordinary world of online dating. He was like a character from one of the indie films they had bonded over—mysterious, alluring, and just out of reach.

THE FIRST DATE

A soft chime from her phone signaled a message, and Julia eagerly picked it up. It was a text from Daniel.

"I'm on my way," he wrote. "I can't wait to see you again."

A smile played on her lips as she typed back a response. "I'm looking forward to it too."

The clock on her wall seemed to move in slow motion as Julia waited for the minutes to pass. She checked her phone obsessively, willing it to ring with another message from Daniel. Her heart raced as she imagined their reunion.

Finally, the moment arrived. There was a knock at the door, and Julia's pulse quickened. She took a deep breath, checked her appearance one last time, and headed for the door.

Opening it, she was greeted by the sight of Daniel, dressed in a tailored suit that accentuated his tall, lean frame. He smiled warmly, his dark eyes filled with a mixture of excitement and anticipation.

"Julia," he said, his voice low and melodic, sending a shiver down her spine. "You look stunning."

She blushed and returned his smile. "Thank you, Daniel. You look quite dashing yourself."

As they stood in the doorway, a sense of familiarity washed over them, as if they had known each other for far longer than a mere week. The connection was undeniable, and it propelled them forward, out into the city streets on their second date.

The night was alive with possibilities as they strolled through the bustling streets, the city's neon lights casting a surreal glow on their surroundings.

They wandered through a maze of winding alleys, discovering hidden gems—a cozy jazz club, a quaint bookshop, and a charming gelato stand.

Their conversation flowed effortlessly, as if they were picking up from where they had left off in the cafe. They talked about their dreams, their past adventures, and the books and films that had shaped their lives. The city seemed to come alive around them, each moment tinged with the electricity of their connection.

As the evening deepened, Daniel led Julia to a rooftop terrace overlooking the city skyline. The view was breathtaking, the city's twinkling lights stretching out in every direction, a sea of possibilities and dreams.

They settled into a corner table, and Julia couldn't help but feel a sense of vulnerability as she gazed into Daniel's eyes. There was an unspoken question hanging in the air—a question that had been growing since the moment they had first connected online.

"Daniel," she began, her voice hesitant, "there's something I've been wondering about."

He met her gaze, his expression open and sincere. "Ask me anything, Julia."

"Why the mystery?" she blurted out. "Why hide behind shadows and enigmatic profiles? What are you searching for in the digital realm?"

For a moment, Daniel's gaze faltered, and Julia wondered if she had crossed a line. But then he sighed, his shoulders relaxing as if a weight had been lifted.

"I suppose it's time I shared the truth with you," he said, his voice soft and filled with a hint of melancholy. "The digital realm offers a sense of anonymity, a chance to explore the depths of human connection without the burden of preconceptions and judgments. I've been searching for something elusive, something that transcends the ordinary."

Julia leaned in closer, captivated by his words. "What is it, Daniel? What are you searching for?"

He looked deep into her eyes, his gaze unwavering. "I'm searching for a connection that defies explanation, a love that exists on a plane beyond the ordinary. I believe that the digital age, for all its flaws, has the potential to bridge the gap between souls, to connect us in ways we never thought possible."

Julia's heart raced as she absorbed his words. There was a vulnerability in his confession, a raw honesty that touched her soul. She realized that she, too, had been searching for something extraordinary in the digital realm—a love that transcended the confines of the ordinary world.

As the night stretched on, Julia and Daniel's conversation deepened, and the world around them seemed to fade into the background. They were two souls on a journey of discovery, navigating the uncharted territory of love in the digital age.

The rooftop terrace was bathed in moonlight, and as they shared stories and dreams, a profound sense of connection grew between them. Julia couldn't deny the magnetic pull she felt toward Daniel, a pull that seemed to defy logic and reason.

As they gazed out at the city skyline, hand in hand, Julia couldn't help but wonder if their connection was the kind of love that Daniel had been searching for—a love that existed in the digital age, a love that was both mysterious and undeniable, a love that had the power to change their lives forever.

The Disappearing Act

The night air was thick with anticipation as Julia and Daniel descended from the rooftop terrace. Their second date had been an enchanting whirlwind of shared stories, laughter, and the kind of connection that left them both feeling exhilarated and alive.

As they walked along the dimly lit streets, Julia's fingers intertwined with Daniel's, the world around them seemed to fade away. They were wrapped in a cocoon of their own making, a world where the digital age had brought them together, and their hearts had forged an unbreakable bond.

"So," Julia began, breaking the comfortable silence between them, "what happens next, Daniel?"

He looked at her, his dark eyes filled with a mixture of vulnerability and determination. "I don't want this to end, Julia. I want to keep exploring this connection, to see where it leads us."

Her heart skipped a beat at his words. "I feel the same way," she confessed, her voice barely above a whisper.

As they continued to walk, the city's neon lights cast long shadows on the sidewalk. Julia couldn't help but wonder about the enigmatic man beside her.

There was still so much she didn't know about Daniel—his past, his secrets, the reasons behind his digital quest for something extraordinary.

The streets became quieter as they ventured into a less populated neighborhood. Julia's apartment was just a few blocks away, and she couldn't deny the temptation to invite Daniel inside. Their connection was undeniable, and the digital world had led them to this moment—a moment that held the promise of something profound.

But as they approached her apartment building, a flicker of doubt crossed Daniel's face. He hesitated at the entrance, his grip on Julia's hand tightening.

"Julia," he said, his voice uncertain, "there's something I need to tell you."

She looked at him, her heart racing. "What is it, Daniel?"

He took a deep breath, his gaze fixed on the ground as if he were choosing his words carefully. "I need to be honest with you. There's a reason I've been so guarded, so mysterious."

Julia's curiosity piqued, and a knot of unease formed in her stomach. "What is it, Daniel? You can tell me."

He met her gaze, his eyes filled with a mixture of regret and determination. "The truth is, Julia, I'm not entirely who I've portrayed myself to be."

Her heart sank as she processed his words. "What do you mean?"

Daniel looked away for a moment before turning back to her. "The photo on my profile, the one you first saw—it's not entirely me. It's a composite image, a mix of different faces."

Julia's mind raced as she tried to make sense of what he was saying. "Why would you do that, Daniel? Why create a fake profile?"

He sighed, and the weight of his confession hung heavy in the air. "I was trying to protect myself, Julia. I've been hurt before, and I wanted to shield my true identity from the unpredictable world of online dating."

Julia felt a surge of anger and confusion. The man she had opened herself up to, the man she had shared her hopes and dreams with, had deceived her. Her trust had been betrayed, and she struggled to find the right words to respond.

"Daniel," she said, her voice trembling, "you can't build a connection based on deception. Trust is the foundation of any relationship."

He nodded, his gaze filled with remorse. "I know, Julia. And I'm truly sorry. But please, hear me out. There's more to the story."

Reluctantly, Julia motioned for him to continue. She needed to understand the full extent of Daniel's deception and what had led him to this point.

He took a deep breath and began to reveal his past. "Several years ago, I met someone online, just like we did. We connected on a deep level, or so I thought. We made plans to meet in person, but when the time came, she disappeared without a trace. It was as if she had never existed."

Julia listened intently, her anger giving way to empathy. She could hear the pain in Daniel's voice, the scars left by a past betrayal that still haunted him.

"I vowed never to let that happen again," he continued. "I decided to create a persona that would protect me from the possibility of being hurt. But then, I met you, Julia, and everything changed."

Tears welled up in Julia's eyes as she realized the depth of Daniel's struggle. He had hidden behind a facade to shield himself from the pain of past wounds, but their connection had breached his defenses, leaving him vulnerable once more.

"I understand why you did it, Daniel," she said softly, her anger replaced by compassion. "But trust goes both ways. You need to trust me too."

He nodded, his eyes filled with gratitude. "I do trust you, Julia. That's why I needed to tell you the truth. I don't want to hide anymore."

As they stood there in the dimly lit entrance of her apartment building, Julia and Daniel faced a pivotal moment in their connection. The digital age had brought them together, but now they were confronted with the challenge of building something real, something based on honesty and trust.

Julia knew that their journey was far from over, that there were still many questions and mysteries to unravel. But as they looked into each other's eyes, she couldn't deny the magnetic pull that had drawn them together, a pull that transcended the complexities of the digital realm and held the promise of something genuine and profound.

Together, they took the first step toward forging a connection that defied explanation, a connection that would lead them down a path filled with challenges and discoveries, a connection that had the power to change their lives in ways they could never have imagined.

Unraveling the Deception

Julia stood in the dimly lit corridor of her apartment building, her mind racing as she tried to process Daniel's confession. The revelation that he had created a composite image for his dating profile had shaken the foundation of trust between them. Yet, his heartfelt explanation had stirred a sense of empathy within her.

"Julia," Daniel said, his voice filled with a mix of hope and apprehension, "I understand if you're angry or disappointed. But please, give me a chance to make things right."

She turned to face him, her heart torn between her growing feelings for Daniel and the sense of betrayal that still lingered. "Daniel, I need time to think about this."

He nodded, his dark eyes filled with understanding. "I'll give you the time you need. Just know that I'm truly sorry for not being honest with you from the start."

As he walked away, Julia watched his retreating figure, a whirlwind of emotions churning within her. She had been drawn to him in a way she had never experienced before, and the connection between them was undeniable. But trust was fragile, and she needed to decide whether she could rebuild it with a man who had started their relationship with deception.

Inside her apartment, Julia sank onto the couch, her thoughts in turmoil. The digital age had brought them together, and yet it had also introduced a layer of complexity and doubt into their budding romance. She couldn't deny that there was something special about Daniel, something that had sparked a fire within her, but she needed to reconcile her feelings with the knowledge of his past actions.

The days that followed were marked by a sense of distance between Julia and Daniel. They continued to exchange messages and occasional phone calls, but the ease and intimacy of their conversations had been replaced by a guardedness that hung in the air like an unspoken question.

Julia immersed herself in her work and daily routines, trying to find clarity amidst the uncertainty. She confided in her close friends, sharing the details of her whirlwind connection with Daniel and the subsequent revelation of his deception. They offered support and advice, but the decision ultimately rested on her shoulders.

One evening, as Julia sat at her desk, her laptop open to the dating app that had brought her and Daniel together, a message notification appeared on the screen. It was from him.

"I miss you, Julia," the message read. "I know I messed up, but I can't stop thinking about you."

Her heart ached as she read his words. There was an authenticity in his message, a vulnerability that echoed the way he had confessed his past. Julia realized that she couldn't ignore the pull she felt toward him, the connection that had transcended the digital realm.

With trembling fingers, she typed out her response. "I miss you too, Daniel.

But we need to talk in person."

He replied almost immediately, his eagerness palpable. "I'll come to your apartment tonight. We can finally have that honest conversation."

Julia hesitated for a moment before agreeing to the meeting. She knew that facing Daniel in person would be challenging, but it was the only way to address the questions and doubts that had arisen between them.

As the evening approached, Julia's heart pounded with anticipation. She had a million questions and uncertainties, but one thing was clear—she needed to understand the depth of Daniel's feelings and whether they could move past the deception that had marked the beginning of their relationship.

The knock on her door came with a mix of excitement and trepidation. Julia opened it to find Daniel standing there, his eyes filled with a mixture of hope and anxiety.

"Julia," he said, his voice barely above a whisper, "thank you for giving me this chance."

She nodded and invited him inside. They settled on the couch, the air heavy with unspoken emotions. It was a moment of truth, a moment that would determine the fate of their connection.

"Daniel," Julia began, her voice steady, "I need to understand why you did what you did. Why create a fake profile?"

He took a deep breath, his gaze fixed on the floor. "It's not an excuse, but it was a defense mechanism. I've been hurt in the past, and I wanted to protect myself from the possibility of being hurt again."

Julia nodded, her heart softening as she recognized the pain in his eyes. "I understand that, Daniel. But trust is essential in a relationship. How can we move forward from here?"

He looked up at her, his expression earnest. "I want to be completely honest with you from now on. I want to build something real, something based on trust and authenticity."

Julia considered his words carefully, the weight of her decision hanging in the air. She knew that rebuilding trust would take time and effort, but there was something about Daniel that she couldn't let go of. He had touched a part of her soul that had long remained dormant.

"Daniel," she said, her voice filled with conviction, "I'm willing to give us a chance. But we have to be open with each other, no more secrets."

He nodded, a sense of relief washing over him. "I promise, Julia, no more secrets."

As they sat there on the couch, the digital age that had brought them together seemed to fade into the background. They were two individuals navigating the complexities of human connection, facing the challenges and uncertainties that love often brought.

The path ahead was uncertain, and there were no guarantees. But as Julia and Daniel looked into each other's eyes, they knew that they were embarking on a journey—a journey filled with the potential for something genuine and profound, a journey that would test their trust and resilience, a journey that had the power to change their lives in ways they could never have imagined.

Digital Detectives

The decision to rebuild trust in her relationship with Daniel was not one Julia took lightly. While she had forgiven him for his initial deception, a shadow of doubt still lingered in the corners of her mind. It was a reminder of the complexity of love in the digital age, where connections could be forged and broken with the tap of a screen.

In the days that followed their heartfelt conversation, Julia and Daniel embarked on a journey to strengthen their connection and honesty. They shared more about their pasts, their hopes for the future, and the lessons they had learned from their previous relationships. Each revelation brought them closer, forging a bond that transcended the virtual realm.

Yet, despite their efforts, a sense of unease remained within Julia. She couldn't shake the feeling that there were still secrets lurking in the digital shadows, mysteries that needed to be unraveled. She confided in her closest friends about her lingering doubts, and they offered their support and advice.

One evening, as Julia sat in her cozy apartment, her laptop open on her dining table, she received an unexpected message from Daniel. "I have something to share with you," it read. "Can we meet tomorrow night?"

The message sent a shiver down Julia's spine. Her curiosity piqued, she agreed to the meeting, arranging to see Daniel at a quiet park near her apartment. The digital age had brought them together, and it seemed that it also held the key to the secrets that still lingered between them.

As she arrived at the park the following evening, a sense of anticipation weighed on her shoulders. The night air was cool and crisp, and the park was bathed in the soft glow of streetlights. She spotted Daniel waiting near a bench, his face illuminated by the soft light of his phone.

"Daniel," she greeted him, her voice filled with a mixture of curiosity and apprehension. "What did you want to share with me?"

He looked at her, his eyes filled with determination. "Julia, I've been doing some digging into my own past, into the secrets I've been hiding. I want to share the truth with you, no matter how difficult it may be."

Julia's heart raced as she listened to his words. She knew that this conversation would be a turning point in their relationship, a moment that would either bring them closer or push them further apart.

They settled on the bench, and Daniel began to reveal his past—a past that held more secrets than she could have imagined.

"I told you about the woman I met online, the one who disappeared without a trace," he began. "Her name was Isabella."

Julia listened intently as he continued, his voice filled with a mixture of sadness and regret. "Isabella and I had connected on a level I had never experienced before. We shared our hopes, our dreams, and our deepest fears. We made plans to meet in person, to take our connection to the next level. But when the day came, she vanished."

He paused, his gaze fixed on the ground. "I was devastated, Julia. It felt as if she had been a mirage, a ghost from the digital realm. I vowed to find out what had happened to her, to uncover the truth behind her disappearance."

Julia couldn't help but feel a sense of empathy for Daniel as he shared his painful past. "What did you discover, Daniel?"

He looked up at her, his eyes filled with determination. "I began to dig into her online presence, searching for any clues that might lead me to her. I discovered that she had used a fake name, a fake identity, just like I had."

Julia's heart skipped a beat as she realized the complexity of the situation. "So, you were both hiding behind fake profiles?"

He nodded, a sense of guilt weighing on him. "Yes, Julia. It was a web of deception, a world where trust was scarce. But I couldn't let it go. I needed to find Isabella, to understand what had driven her to disappear."

As Daniel continued his story, Julia began to piece together the puzzle of their shared past. It was a world where digital connections and hidden identities had collided, leaving a trail of secrets and unanswered questions.

"I finally managed to track down a lead," Daniel said, his voice filled with urgency. "I discovered that Isabella had been involved in something dangerous, something that had forced her to go into hiding. I tried to follow the breadcrumbs, to uncover the truth, but the trail went cold."

Julia's mind raced as she absorbed his words. The story of Isabella's disappearance was like something out of a suspense novel, a tale of hidden identities and a perilous digital world. She couldn't help but wonder how it had all connected to her own journey with Daniel.

"What does this have to do with us?" she asked, her voice trembling.

Daniel's gaze met hers, his eyes filled with a sense of resolution. "I realized that my search for Isabella had led me to you, Julia. Our paths crossed in the digital realm, and I couldn't ignore the connection we shared. I wanted to find answers not only for Isabella but also for us—to understand what had drawn us together."

Julia was stunned by the revelation. The digital age had brought them together in ways she could never have imagined. Their connection had been shaped by the secrets and mysteries of their shared pasts, a past that was still shrouded in uncertainty.

"Daniel," she said, her voice filled with emotion, "we need to find out what happened to Isabella, to uncover the truth behind her disappearance. Only then can we move forward."

He nodded, a sense of determination in his eyes. "I agree, Julia. We'll embark on this journey together, as digital detectives, to unravel the mysteries of our past and secure a future built on trust and honesty."

As they sat in the quiet park, the digital age that had brought them together seemed to take on a new significance. Julia and Daniel were no longer passive participants in the digital realm—they were active agents in a story of suspense, intrigue, and discovery.

Their journey had only just begun, and the path ahead was uncertain. But as they looked into each other's eyes, they knew that they were bound by a connection that defied explanation, a connection that had the power to uncover the truth and change their lives in ways they could never have imagined.

The Trail of Secrets

Julia and Daniel's decision to unravel the mysteries of their shared past marked the beginning of a new chapter in their relationship. They had become digital detectives, determined to uncover the truth behind the disappearance of Isabella—the woman who had drawn them together in a world of hidden identities and secrets.

Their first step in this enigmatic journey was to gather information about Isabella, whose real identity remained shrouded in mystery. With Daniel's guidance, Julia began to delve into the digital breadcrumbs left behind by Isabella, searching for any clue that might lead them closer to the truth.

Late one evening, Julia sat at her dining table, her laptop open in front of her. She had created a digital investigation board, a collage of photos, maps, and notes that documented their progress. The room was bathed in the soft glow of the screen as she typed away.

"Isabella's online presence is like a labyrinth," Daniel remarked, his voice filled with a mixture of frustration and determination. "But I'm certain that there are clues out there waiting to be discovered."

Julia nodded, her fingers flying across the keyboard. She had already uncovered several online accounts associated with the name Isabella, but each one seemed to lead to a dead end. They needed more information, something tangible to follow.

As days turned into weeks, their investigation grew more complex. They discovered that Isabella had been active on multiple social media platforms, using different aliases and profiles. She had left behind a trail of digital footprints, each one revealing a different facet of her life.

"I found a blog post she wrote a few years ago," Julia said, her voice tinged with excitement. "It's about her passion for travel and adventure. Maybe there's a clue hidden within her writings."

Daniel leaned closer to the screen, his eyes scanning the blog post. "She mentions a place called 'The Whispering Woods' in the post. I've never heard of it before. It could be a clue."

They decided to focus their investigation on this mysterious location, hoping that it would lead them closer to Isabella's whereabouts and the truth behind her disappearance. Julia's digital sleuthing skills were put to the test as she scoured the internet for any mention of "The Whispering Woods."

Late one night, as Julia scrolled through a travel forum, she stumbled upon a thread that piqued her interest. It was titled "The Enigma of The Whispering Woods," and the discussion was filled with rumors and stories about the supposedly haunted forest.

"The locals say that strange things happen in The Whispering Woods," one user wrote. "People have reported hearing voices, whispers in the wind that seem to carry secrets."

Another post mentioned a local legend that had been passed down through generations. "They say that the forest holds the key to hidden truths, that those who venture deep into its heart may uncover long-buried secrets."

Julia couldn't help but feel a sense of excitement. "Daniel, I think we need to visit The Whispering Woods. It might be the key to unraveling Isabella's secrets."

He nodded in agreement, a glint of determination in his eyes. "We'll go together, Julia. We'll follow the trail of secrets and find the answers we've been searching for."

In the days that followed, Julia and Daniel made preparations for their journey into The Whispering Woods. They packed backpacks filled with essentials, including flashlights, maps, and notebooks. The forest was located a few hours' drive from the city, and they planned to spend the weekend exploring its depths.

As they entered the forest, a sense of mystery and anticipation hung in the air. The towering trees created a canopy that filtered the sunlight, casting dappled shadows on the forest floor. The air was filled with the faint rustling of leaves and the distant murmur of a creek.

They followed a winding trail deeper into the woods, their footsteps echoing in the silence. Julia couldn't help but feel a sense of unease, as if they were walking into the unknown, pursuing a truth that might be better left undiscovered.

Hours passed as they ventured further into the forest, the daylight gradually fading. They decided to set up camp for the night, pitching their tent in a small clearing. The forest seemed to come alive as darkness descended, with strange whispers carried on the wind.

As they sat by the campfire, Julia and Daniel shared stories of their own secrets and fears. They talked about the uncertainties of life, the choices they had made, and the paths that had led them to this moment. The forest around them seemed to absorb their words, as if it held secrets of its own.

Suddenly, a chilling breeze swept through the clearing, causing the flames of their campfire to flicker and dance. Julia shivered, a feeling of unease washing over her.

"Did you hear that?" she asked, her voice barely above a whisper.

Daniel's eyes darted around the darkness. "I heard something, too. It sounded like a whisper."

They strained their ears, trying to catch any hint of the mysterious voices that had been mentioned in the online forum. The forest seemed to hold its breath, as if waiting for them to uncover its secrets.

And then, in the stillness of the night, they heard it—a faint, ethereal whisper carried on the breeze. It was indistinct, like a secret too fragile to be spoken aloud.

Julia and Daniel exchanged a look, their hearts pounding in their chests. They knew that they were on the cusp of a revelation, that the forest held the key to Isabella's secrets.

With flashlights in hand, they followed the whispers, their beams of light cutting through the darkness. The forest seemed to come alive around them, the leaves rustling in response to their presence. It was as if the very trees were guiding them toward a hidden truth.

The whispers grew louder, more distinct, as they ventured deeper into the heart of The Whispering Woods. Julia and Daniel exchanged words of encouragement, a shared determination to uncover the secrets that had eluded them for so long.

And then, they stumbled upon it—a hidden clearing deep within the forest, illuminated by the pale light of the moon. In the center of the clearing stood a solitary tree, its branches reaching skyward like gnarled fingers.

As they approached the tree, they realized that it was unlike any other they had seen in the forest. The bark was etched with symbols and markings, and at its base lay a weathered journal, its pages filled with handwritten notes.

Julia picked up the journal, her hands trembling. "This must be it, Daniel—the key to Isabella's secrets."

Together, they began to read the notes, uncovering a tale of love, betrayal, and the pursuit of hidden truths. The journal told the story of Isabella's own journey into The Whispering Woods, her quest to uncover the secrets that had haunted her family for generations.

As they read, Julia and Daniel felt a profound connection to Isabella, a woman whose digital presence had drawn them together. They realized that her disappearance had been driven by a desire to uncover the truth, a desire that had brought them to this very moment.

As the night wore on, Julia and Daniel continued to read the journal, their hearts heavy with the weight of Isabella's story. They knew that they were standing on the precipice of a revelation, a truth that had the power to change everything.

The forest around them

seemed to listen, the whispers in the wind growing more insistent. Julia and Daniel were no longer just digital detectives—they were the keepers of a secret, the guardians of a story that had been hidden in the heart of The Whispering Woods.

And as they read the final pages of the journal, they realized that their journey was far from over. The digital age had brought them together, but it was their shared pursuit of truth that had bound them in a way that transcended the virtual realm.

Together, they would follow the trail of secrets, uncover the mysteries of Isabella's past, and secure a future built on trust, honesty, and the profound connection they had forged. The digital age had given them a path to each other, and now it had led them to a destiny intertwined with a forest that whispered secrets in the night.

The Unraveling Truth

Julia and Daniel sat in the moonlit clearing of The Whispering Woods, the journal containing Isabella's secrets resting in Julia's hands. The forest around them seemed to hold its breath, as if awaiting their next move. The weight of the revelations they had uncovered bore down on them, a sense of destiny pulling them deeper into the enigma of Isabella's past.

"We need to keep reading," Daniel said, his voice filled with determination. "We can't stop now. Isabella's story holds the key to everything."

Julia nodded in agreement, and together they continued to read the journal's pages. Isabella's words painted a vivid picture of her quest for truth, her determination to uncover the mysteries that had haunted her family for generations.

Isabella had learned of a hidden family secret—a legend passed down through the ages. It spoke of a hidden treasure, a legacy that had been lost to time. Isabella's ancestors had been keepers of this secret, protectors of a truth that had the power to change everything.

As Julia and Daniel delved deeper into the journal, they discovered that Isabella had believed that the key to unlocking this secret lay within The Whispering Woods. She had embarked on a perilous journey into the forest, determined to find the answers that had eluded her family for so long.

But as the journal chronicled Isabella's adventures in the forest, it became clear that she had encountered obstacles and dangers she had not anticipated. The whispers that had drawn Julia and Daniel deeper into the woods were not mere echoes of the wind—they were the voices of those who had sought the treasure before her, voices that seemed to both guide and warn her.

One entry in the journal stood out—a description of a hidden cavern within the forest, a place where Isabella believed the truth was concealed. The journal hinted at a series of puzzles and riddles that guarded the entrance to the cavern, challenges that had thwarted her progress.

"We need to find this hidden cavern," Julia said, her voice filled with determination. "It's where Isabella believed the treasure and the truth were hidden."

Daniel nodded, his gaze fixed on the moonlit forest. "But we need to be careful, Julia. Isabella's journey was fraught with danger. We don't know what awaits us in that cavern."

As they closed the journal and prepared to leave the clearing, they couldn't shake the feeling that they were being watched. The whispers of the forest seemed to intensify, a chorus of voices both haunting and beckoning.

The journey back through the darkened woods was filled with an eerie sense of foreboding. The trees seemed to close in around them, their branches twisting like gnarled fingers, and the whispers grew louder, as if the very forest itself were conspiring to keep its secrets hidden.

Eventually, they emerged from the woods, the moonlight guiding their way back to their campsite. They packed their belongings and made their way back to the city, a sense of urgency driving them forward.

Back in the city, Julia and Daniel continued their digital investigation into the hidden cavern within The Whispering Woods. They pored over maps, researched local legends, and pieced together the clues left by Isabella in her journal.

One day, while studying a map of the forest, Julia noticed a pattern—a series of symbols and markings that corresponded to Isabella's description of the hidden cavern. It was as if the forest itself had been trying to guide them to the truth.

"We need to go back to The Whispering Woods," Julia said, her voice filled with a sense of purpose. "I think we're close to finding the hidden cavern."

Daniel agreed, and they made plans to return to the forest, armed with the knowledge they had gathered and a determination to unravel the final mystery that had brought them together.

As they entered the forest once more, a sense of anticipation hung in the air. The whispers seemed to greet them, as if acknowledging their return. Julia and Daniel followed the markings and symbols, navigating the labyrinthine trails of The Whispering Woods.

Hours passed as they ventured deeper into the forest, the daylight gradually fading. They knew they were drawing closer to the hidden cavern, and the air was charged with a sense of electricity, a feeling that they were on the cusp of a revelation.

And then, they found it—a massive stone door concealed within the heart of the forest, covered in symbols and engravings that mirrored those in Isabella's journal. The entrance to the hidden cavern had been found.

As they approached the stone door, a feeling of trepidation washed over them. They knew that the challenges and puzzles described in Isabella's journal lay ahead, guarding the entrance to the truth they sought.

Julia and Daniel began to decipher the symbols and markings on the door, working together to unlock the mysteries that had eluded Isabella. Each puzzle they solved brought them closer to their goal, and their determination grew stronger with each passing moment.

Finally, the massive stone door creaked open, revealing the entrance to the hidden cavern. The air within was cool and musty, and the glow of their flashlights illuminated a chamber filled with ancient artifacts and relics.

But at the heart of the cavern, they found what they had been searching for—a chest, covered in ornate carvings and symbols, its lid sealed shut. It was the treasure that Isabella had sought, the legacy that had been lost to time.

As Julia and Daniel opened the chest, their breath caught in their throats. Inside, they found a collection of documents and letters, each one containing a piece of the puzzle—a map, a diary, and a letter that revealed the truth.

The truth was a revelation that left them both stunned. It was a secret that had been hidden for generations, a truth that had the power to change the course of history.

As they read the letter, written by one of Isabella's ancestors, they realized that the legacy of their family had been tied to a secret organization, a group that had sought to protect a powerful artifact—an artifact that had the ability to change the world.

Julia and Daniel understood the weight of their discovery, the responsibility that had been thrust upon them. They were now the guardians of a secret that had been hidden for centuries, a secret that had been sought by many but had remained elusive until now.

Their journey had brought them together in ways they could never have imagined. The digital age had led them to a destiny intertwined with the secrets of The Whispering Woods, a destiny that would test their resolve and their trust in each other.

As they left the hidden cavern, the whispers of the forest seemed to echo in their ears, a reminder of the mysteries that still lay beyond the digital realm. Julia and Daniel knew that their journey was far from over, that they were bound by a connection that defied explanation, a connection that had the power to uncover the truth and change their lives in ways they could never have imagined.

The digital age had given them a path to each other, and now it had led them to a destiny intertwined with a secret that had been hidden for centuries. Together, they would face the challenges and uncertainties that lay ahead, as guardians of a truth that had the power to shape the future.

The Pursuit of Power

The discovery of the hidden cavern in The Whispering Woods had unlocked a mystery that spanned generations, a truth that had the power to change the course of history. Julia and Daniel stood at the precipice of a new chapter in their journey, their hearts filled with a mixture of awe and trepidation.

The documents they had found in the chest within the cavern revealed a secret organization known as "The Custodians." This group had been entrusted with safeguarding a powerful artifact—an artifact of unknown origin and unimaginable capabilities. It was this artifact that had drawn Isabella into the depths of the forest and had ultimately led Julia and Daniel to their destiny.

As they examined the maps and documents, they realized that the artifact's whereabouts were still unknown. Isabella's journal had hinted at the existence of a map that could lead to its discovery, but that map remained elusive.

"We need to find this map," Julia said, her voice filled with determination. "It's the key to locating the artifact and uncovering the full extent of the truth."

Daniel nodded in agreement, his gaze fixed on the documents spread out before them. "But we have to be careful, Julia. The Custodians have guarded this secret for centuries. There may be others who are still searching for the artifact."

The realization that they were not alone in their pursuit weighed heavily on their minds. Julia and Daniel knew that they had stumbled upon a world of intrigue and danger, a world where the pursuit of power was a driving force.

They began their investigation into The Custodians, piecing together fragments of information from the documents they had found. The organization had a long history, dating back to the ancient world, and had played a pivotal role in shaping the course of events throughout history.

The Custodians had been entrusted with the artifact by a mysterious figure known as the "Guardian," whose true identity remained a closely guarded secret. The artifact was said to possess the power to control the elements, to shape the destiny of nations, and to grant its possessor unimaginable power.

As Julia and Daniel delved deeper into The Custodians' history, they uncovered a trail of intrigue and betrayal. The organization had faced internal divisions and external threats, with factions vying for control of the artifact and its power.

One name kept recurring in their research—a figure known as "The Seeker." The Seeker had been a relentless pursuer of the artifact, driven by a thirst for power and a belief that it held the key to unlocking the secrets of the universe.

Julia and Daniel knew that they needed to find the map that would lead them to the artifact before The Seeker or any other interested party could lay their hands on it. Their journey had become a race against time, a race to secure a truth that had remained hidden for centuries.

They returned to The Whispering Woods, determined to follow the clues left by Isabella in her journal. The forest seemed to welcome them, its whispers guiding them toward their next destination. As they ventured deeper into the woods, they stumbled upon a hidden grove, its center dominated by a massive stone pedestal.

On the pedestal, they found a plaque inscribed with cryptic symbols and markings, the same symbols that had appeared in the documents they had discovered. It was a puzzle, a riddle that held the key to their quest.

Julia and Daniel began to decipher the symbols, working together to unlock the pedestal's secrets. It was a challenging task, requiring both their intellect and their intuition. Each correct combination of symbols brought them one step closer to unraveling the mystery.

Hours passed, the daylight fading as they continued to work tirelessly. Finally, as the last rays of sunlight vanished, they heard a soft click—the pedestal had unlocked.

With bated breath, Julia and Daniel turned the pedestal to reveal a hidden compartment. Inside, they found a parchment, yellowed with age, and a map that depicted a route through The Whispering Woods.

"This is it," Julia whispered, her voice filled with awe. "The map that will lead us to the artifact."

They carefully examined the map, its markings indicating a path through the forest that would ultimately lead to their destination. It was a path that had been followed by Isabella, a path that had drawn them closer to the truth.

With the map in hand, Julia and Daniel embarked on their journey deeper into The Whispering Woods, following the path that had been laid out for them. The forest seemed to come alive around them, as if it were guiding their way, and the whispers grew louder, as if encouraging them to continue.

As they journeyed through the night, their flashlights cutting through the darkness, they realized that they were not alone in their pursuit. The Seeker had discovered their trail and was hot on their heels, driven by a relentless determination to obtain the artifact's power.

Julia and Daniel's hearts pounded with a mixture of fear and determination as they continued to follow the map. They knew that they were drawing closer to their goal, that the artifact and the truth were within their reach.

And then, as the first light of dawn broke through the trees, they stumbled upon it—the artifact. It was nestled within a stone alcove, its surface adorned with ancient symbols and markings that seemed to pulse with energy.

As they approached the artifact, a sense of awe washed over them. They realized that they were standing in the presence of something extraordinary, something that had the power to shape the destiny of nations and individuals alike.

But their moment of awe was short-lived, for The Seeker emerged from the shadows, his eyes filled with a hunger for power. He had finally caught up to them, and he would stop at nothing to obtain the artifact.

A tense standoff ensued, with Julia, Daniel, and The Seeker facing off in the heart of The Whispering Woods. The artifact stood between them, a symbol of power and destiny.

"You can't have it," Julia said, her voice filled with determination. "The artifact belongs to no one. It must be protected."

The Seeker's laughter echoed through the forest, a chilling sound that sent shivers down their spines. "Protect it? No, my dear. I intend to harness its power, to shape the world according to my desires."

With a sudden burst of energy, The Seeker lunged for the artifact, his hand reaching out to grasp it. But Julia and Daniel acted quickly, using the map they had found to unlock the artifact's protective mechanisms.

As they worked together to safeguard the artifact, a brilliant light enveloped them, filling the forest with a blinding radiance. The Seeker screamed in frustration and pain as he was repelled by the artifact's energy, forced to retreat into the darkness.

When the light subsided, Julia and Daniel found themselves alone in the grove, the artifact now secured and protected. They had prevailed against The Seeker, but they knew that their journey was far from over.

The digital age had brought them together, had led them on a path to uncover a truth that had been hidden for centuries. Julia and Daniel had become guardians of a secret that held the power to shape the world, a secret that would test their resolve and their trust in each other.

As they looked at the artifact before them, they realized that their destiny was intertwined with its power, a destiny that would carry them forward into a world of intrigue and danger, a world where the pursuit of power would be a driving force.

The digital age had given

them a path to each other, and now it had led them to a destiny intertwined with a secret that had the power to change everything. Together, they would face the challenges and uncertainties that lay ahead, as guardians of a truth that had the power to shape the future.

The Unveiling

With the artifact secured and The Seeker vanquished, Julia and Daniel returned to the city, their minds filled with a sense of awe and trepidation. The artifact was now in their possession, a source of unimaginable power that had the potential to change the course of history.

Their journey had become a race against time, as they knew that others would still be searching for the artifact, driven by a relentless hunger for its power. Julia and Daniel realized that they needed to unlock the secrets of the artifact, to understand its true nature and purpose, before it fell into the wrong hands.

As they examined the artifact in the dim light of their apartment, they were struck by its beauty and complexity. Its surface was adorned with intricate symbols and markings, and its shape seemed to shift and change with each passing moment.

"We need to find a way to unlock its power," Julia said, her voice filled with determination. "We have the artifact, but we don't yet understand how to harness its capabilities."

Daniel nodded, his gaze fixed on the artifact. "Isabella's journal mentioned that the artifact was tied to a series of rituals and incantations. We need to decipher these rituals and unlock the artifact's true potential."

Their research into the rituals and incantations proved to be a challenging task. The documents they had found in the hidden cavern contained fragments of information, hints and clues that hinted at the artifact's purpose but did not provide a clear path forward.

They delved into ancient texts and scrolls, searching for clues that would help them decipher the mysteries of the artifact. It was a painstaking process, requiring both their intellect and their intuition.

Days turned into weeks as they continued their research, their determination undiminished. They worked tirelessly, pouring over texts and documents, piecing together the fragments of information they had gathered.

And then, one fateful night, as Julia was examining an ancient manuscript, she stumbled upon a revelation—a passage that described a ritual that would unlock the artifact's power. It was a complex series of steps, involving symbols, incantations, and a precise sequence of actions.

Excitement coursed through Julia as she shared her discovery with Daniel. "I think I've found it, Daniel—the ritual that will unlock the artifact's power."

They wasted no time in preparing for the ritual, gathering the necessary materials and making the necessary preparations. The artifact sat before them, its surface pulsing with an otherworldly energy, as if it were waiting to be awakened.

As they began to perform the ritual, they felt a surge of energy coursing through them, a connection to something greater than themselves. Symbols glowed on the artifact's surface, and the air seemed to hum with power.

The incantations they recited filled the room, their voices blending together in a harmonious chant. It was a moment of profound significance, a moment that held the potential to change everything.

And then, as the final incantation was spoken, the artifact erupted in a blinding burst of light. The room was filled with a dazzling radiance, and Julia and Daniel shielded their eyes from the brilliance.

When the light subsided, they found themselves standing before an open portal—a doorway to another realm. It was a world bathed in colors and energies they could scarcely comprehend, a world that beckoned to them with an irresistible pull.

Without hesitation, Julia and Daniel stepped through the portal, their hearts filled with a sense of adventure and purpose. They found themselves in a realm unlike anything they had ever imagined, a place where the laws of reality seemed to bend and shift.

As they explored this otherworldly realm, they realized that it held the key to unlocking the full potential of the artifact. The rituals and incantations they had performed had connected them to this realm, had given them access to its secrets.

They encountered beings of light and energy, entities that seemed to exist beyond the boundaries of time and space. These beings offered guidance and wisdom, helping Julia and Daniel to understand the true nature of the artifact and its power.

The artifact, they learned, was a conduit to the energies of the universe, a bridge between the digital realm and the realms of the unknown. It held the power to shape reality itself, to bring dreams and desires to life.

But with this power came great responsibility. Julia and Daniel realized that they were the guardians of the artifact, entrusted with the task of using its power wisely and for the greater good. They understood that the artifact's true purpose was not to grant them personal power, but to serve as a force for positive change in the world.

Their time in the otherworldly realm was both enlightening and transformative. They gained knowledge and insights that transcended the limitations of the digital age, and they forged a deeper connection to each other and to the artifact.

As they prepared to return to their own world, they knew that their journey was far from over. The digital age had brought them together, had led them on a path to uncover a truth that had been hidden for centuries. They had become guardians of a secret that held the power to shape the destiny of nations and individuals alike.

The artifact had become a symbol of their shared destiny, a destiny that would carry them forward into a world of intrigue and danger, a world where the pursuit of power would be a driving force.

But Julia and Daniel were now armed with knowledge and purpose. They had unlocked the secrets of the artifact, and they were ready to face the challenges and uncertainties that lay ahead, as guardians of a truth that had the power to shape the future.

As they stepped back through the portal and returned to their own world, they knew that they were bound by a connection that defied explanation, a connection that had the power to change everything. The digital age had given them a path to each other, and now it had led them to a destiny intertwined with a power that could shape the world. Together, they would embrace their role as guardians of the artifact, as stewards of a truth that had the potential to bring about a brighter future for all.

The Balance of Power

Julia and Daniel had returned from the otherworldly realm with newfound knowledge and a deep sense of purpose. They were now the guardians of the artifact—a source of incredible power that had the potential to shape reality itself. Their journey had led them to this pivotal moment, and they were determined to use the artifact's power wisely and responsibly.

Back in their apartment, they carefully placed the artifact in a secure case, shielding it from prying eyes. They knew that its existence must remain a closely guarded secret, as there were those who would stop at nothing to obtain it. The memory of The Seeker's relentless pursuit still haunted their thoughts.

Their research into the artifact continued, as they sought to understand its full potential and the responsibilities that came with it. The artifact seemed to respond to their presence, glowing with an inner light that mirrored their own connection to the otherworldly realm.

But with great power came great responsibility, and Julia and Daniel knew that they needed guidance. They reached out to the beings they had encountered in the otherworldly realm, seeking their wisdom and counsel.

As they performed rituals and incantations to commune with these beings, they felt a profound connection to the energies of the universe. Their minds expanded, and they were granted insights and knowledge that transcended the boundaries of human understanding.

The beings spoke of balance and harmony, of the need to use the artifact's power to bring about positive change in the world. They warned against the temptation to seek personal gain or control, emphasizing the importance of humility and empathy.

Julia and Daniel realized that their role as guardians of the artifact was not one of dominance, but of stewardship. They were entrusted with the responsibility of maintaining the delicate balance between the digital realm and the realms of the unknown.

Their newfound knowledge deepened their connection to each other, as they shared a sense of purpose and a commitment to use the artifact's power for the greater good. They knew that they were bound by a destiny that went beyond the digital age, a destiny that had the power to shape the world.

But the world was not without its challenges, and as Julia and Daniel continued their research, they became aware of a growing threat—an organization known as "The Enclave." The Enclave was a shadowy group that sought to control the artifact's power for their own purposes, with no regard for the consequences.

The Enclave's resources and reach were vast, and they would stop at nothing to obtain the artifact. Julia and Daniel realized that they needed to stay one step ahead of their adversaries, to protect the artifact and the knowledge they had gained.

Their research led them to a hidden enclave, a place where The Enclave conducted their clandestine operations. Julia and Daniel knew that they needed to infiltrate this stronghold, to gather information and disrupt their plans.

With a plan in place, they set out on a dangerous mission to penetrate The Enclave's defenses. The digital age had given them the tools and knowledge they needed, and they used their skills to bypass security systems and surveillance.

As they entered the hidden enclave, a sense of danger and anticipation hung in the air. The compound was a labyrinth of corridors and chambers, guarded by enforcers who would stop at nothing to protect their secrets.

Julia and Daniel moved silently through the shadows, their hearts pounding as they neared their objective—a central chamber where The Enclave's leaders held their meetings. They knew that obtaining information from this chamber was the key to unraveling The Enclave's plans.

Using their digital skills, they hacked into the chamber's security system, gaining access to the audio and visual feed. What they witnessed sent shivers down their spines.

The Enclave's leaders were discussing their plans for the artifact, their intentions to harness its power for their own gain. They spoke of a world shaped according to their desires, a world where they held absolute control.

But Julia and Daniel also heard whispers of dissent within The Enclave's ranks, of members who questioned the morality of their actions. It was a glimmer of hope, a potential weakness that could be exploited.

As they continued to monitor The Enclave's discussions, they uncovered a key piece of information—an upcoming meeting that would bring together The Enclave's top leaders. It was an opportunity they couldn't afford to miss, a chance to gather vital information and disrupt The Enclave's plans.

Julia and Daniel devised a plan to infiltrate the meeting, using their digital skills to impersonate Enclave members and gain access to the highly secure location. The day of the meeting arrived, and their hearts raced as they entered the compound, their faces hidden behind masks and disguises.

Inside the meeting room, they listened intently as The Enclave's leaders discussed their strategies and objectives. But their presence did not go unnoticed, and suspicion grew among the members.

With their cover on the verge of being blown, Julia and Daniel made a daring move. They activated a device they had brought with them, projecting a holographic image that disrupted the meeting and created chaos in the room.

In the ensuing confusion, they seized the opportunity to steal documents and data that revealed The Enclave's plans and operations. With the stolen information in hand, they made a hasty exit, narrowly escaping capture.

Back in their apartment, they analyzed the stolen data, uncovering a web of intrigue and deception that went far deeper than they had imagined. The Enclave's reach extended to powerful figures and organizations across the world, and their plans were ambitious and far-reaching.

Julia and Daniel knew that they needed to act quickly to disrupt The Enclave's operations and prevent them from obtaining the artifact. They reached out to the beings they had encountered in the otherworldly realm, seeking their guidance and assistance.

The beings spoke of a ritual—a ritual that would harness the artifact's power to create a protective barrier, shielding it from The Enclave's reach. It was a dangerous and complex undertaking, but Julia and Daniel were willing to take the risk.

With the guidance of the beings and their own unwavering determination, they performed the ritual, channeling the artifact's energy to create a barrier that would safeguard it from The Enclave's influence.

As the ritual reached its climax, a brilliant light enveloped the artifact, and a powerful force field surrounded it. Julia and Daniel knew that they had succeeded, that the artifact was now protected from The Enclave's reach.

But their actions had not gone unnoticed, and The Enclave was quick to retaliate. They launched a series of cyberattacks and threats, seeking to intimidate Julia and Daniel into surrendering the artifact.

The digital age had brought them together, had led them on a path to uncover a truth that had been hidden for centuries. Julia and Daniel had become guardians of a secret that held the power to shape the destiny of nations and individuals alike.

Their journey had tested their resolve and their trust in each other, but they were determined to protect the artifact and its potential for positive change. They knew that their destiny was intertwined with a power that could shape the world, and they were ready to face the challenges and uncertainties that lay ahead.

As they looked at the protected artifact before them, they realized that they were bound by a connection that defied explanation, a connection that had the power to change everything. The digital age had given them a path to each other, and now it had led them to a destiny intertwined with the balance of power, a destiny that would

shape the future. Together, they would embrace their role as guardians of the artifact, as stewards of a truth that had the potential to bring about a brighter future for all.

The Final Confrontation

The protective barrier around the artifact stood as a testament to Julia and Daniel's resolve to safeguard its power. The Enclave had been thwarted, their efforts to obtain the artifact halted by the force field that encircled it. But Julia and Daniel knew that the battle was far from over.

The Enclave was not a foe to be underestimated. Their reach extended across the globe, and their resources were vast. The stolen information had revealed a network of operatives and assets that could be deployed at a moment's notice.

As Julia and Daniel continued to analyze the stolen data, they uncovered a troubling truth. The Enclave's leaders had not been deterred by the failure of their recent meeting; instead, they had intensified their efforts to obtain the artifact.

It was clear that The Enclave viewed the artifact as the key to achieving their ambitions, as a source of power that would grant them control over the digital realm and the real world. They were willing to stop at nothing to obtain it, and Julia and Daniel knew that they needed to stay one step ahead.

Their research led them to a remote location—an underground facility that had once belonged to The Enclave but had been abandoned. It was a place shrouded in mystery, a place where The Enclave had conducted experiments and tests on the artifact.

Julia and Daniel believed that this facility held the key to understanding the full extent of the artifact's capabilities and The Enclave's plans. They prepared for a dangerous mission to infiltrate the facility, knowing that the risks were high.

Their journey took them to the outskirts of a desolate town, where the entrance to the underground facility was hidden beneath a dilapidated warehouse. As they descended into the depths of the facility, they felt a sense of unease that grew with each step.

The facility was a maze of darkened corridors and chambers, the air heavy with the weight of untold secrets. It was clear that The Enclave had gone to great lengths to conceal their activities here.

As Julia and Daniel ventured deeper into the facility, they uncovered evidence of The Enclave's experiments on the artifact. The walls were adorned with schematics and diagrams, each one detailing a different aspect of the artifact's power.

But the true horror of the facility became apparent as they reached the heart of the complex—a chamber that held a series of containment units. Inside these units were beings of pure energy, entities that had been harnessed and imprisoned by The Enclave's experiments.

Julia and Daniel's hearts ached at the sight of these beings, their energies drained and their identities stripped away. It was clear that The Enclave had sought to harness the artifact's power by imprisoning these entities and siphoning their energy.

As they continued to explore the facility, they discovered a central control

THE FINAL CONFRONTATION

room, where The Enclave had monitored their experiments on the artifact. It was here that they uncovered a shocking revelation—a plan to merge the energies of the artifact with a massive network of digital devices, a plan that would grant The Enclave unprecedented power and control.

Realizing the urgency of the situation, Julia and Daniel knew that they needed to put an end to The Enclave's plans once and for all. They activated a series of explosives they had brought with them, setting a countdown in motion to destroy the facility and the artifacts they had created.

With time running out, they made their escape from the facility, racing against the clock to reach the surface. The ground shook as explosions echoed through the tunnels, and debris rained down around them.

As they emerged from the facility, they watched in horror as the entrance collapsed, sealing the underground complex forever. The Enclave's plans had been thwarted, and the beings imprisoned within the facility were finally free.

But the victory came at a cost, as the artifacts created by The Enclave had been destroyed in the process. Julia and Daniel knew that they had made a difficult choice, but it was one that had been necessary to protect the artifact and prevent it from falling into the wrong hands.

Their actions had sent a clear message to The Enclave—that they were willing to do whatever it took to safeguard the artifact and its power. The Enclave had been dealt a significant blow, but Julia and Daniel knew that they could not afford to become complacent.

As they returned to their apartment, they continued to monitor The Enclave's activities, aware that the organization was far from defeated. The battle for control of the artifact had entered a new phase, one where the stakes were higher than ever.

Their journey had tested their resolve and their trust in each other, but they were determined to protect the artifact and its potential for positive change. They knew that their destiny was intertwined with a power that could shape the world, and they were ready to face the challenges and uncertainties that lay ahead.

The digital age had brought them together, had led them on a path to uncover a truth that had been hidden for centuries. Julia and Daniel had become guardians of a secret that held the power to shape the destiny of nations and individuals alike.

As they looked at the protected artifact before them, they realized that they were bound by a connection that defied explanation, a connection that had the power to change everything. The digital age had given them a path to each other, and now it had led them to a destiny intertwined with the balance of power, a destiny that would shape the future.

Together, they would embrace their role as guardians of the artifact, as stewards of a truth that had the potential to bring about a brighter future for all.

www.ingramcontent.com/pod-product-compliance
Lightning Source LLC
LaVergne TN
LVHW050027080526
838202LV00069B/6941

*9 7 8 5 3 7 1 8 6 5 9 0 8 *